The ♥ of Satisfaction

The Power of The Emotional Connection in Sales, Service & Life!

Rich Hand

Copyright © 2016 Hand Written Productions

All rights reserved.

ISBN-10:6589799
ISBN-13:978-1537796932

DEDICATION

To the dedicated Hospice professionals I have had the honor to know, serve with, and to marry! Your special hearts filled with love, caring and tenderness inspire me. You have the most difficult but rewarding job to have been blessed as the caretakers of people knowing they are about to die. You comfort, respect, and value people in a way that provides dignity to those in their greatest time of need. I love you for making heartfelt emotional connections with patients, and the people that love them. I am proud to be among you in a very small way. Keep caring, the world needs more of you!

Rich Hand

"Emotional connections are at the heart of creating an excellent customer experience and a successful life!"

Rich Hand
Author, Speaker, Songwriter, Trainer

"In his latest book, Rich demonstrates how agents and leaders can do what needs to be done to create an excellent customer experience, make the sale, and connect with people. He does it in plain English, and explains why it is so important to connect with the customer. It's a quick read, and one you'll want for every member of your leadership and front line support team."

Phil Gerbyshak*, Speaker, author of *Make It Great*, and his newest effort, *Leadership Gone Social

CONTENTS

	Acknowledgments	i
1	Preface	9
2	Introduction	15
3	The Behaviors That Lead to an Emotional Connection	26
4	Empathy, Genuine, Honesty…	27
5	Becoming an Emotional Connector	59
6	Personality Types and Why it Matters in Emotional Connections	61
7	Making Emotional Connections	69
8	Emotional Connections in Sales	70
9	Emotional Connections in Service	88
10	Conclusion	110
11	About the Author	112

Rich Hand

ACKNOWLEDGMENTS

The ability to impact people in a positive way is a gift. I have been a life-long learner with a passion for understanding human behavior to make better connections. I have observed countless people with the gift of making emotional connections. I could never document them all, it would take all of the pages of this book. A few people that stand out are my Mom, Anne P. Hand, who dedicated her life to making people feel special. Sophie Klossner who I worked with for many years as Executive Director of Membership at HDI. She showed me the value of a hug in the "corporate" world. All of my Aunts and Uncles who provided me with excellent models to follow. Mike Perkins, a successful salesman that can light up a room, entertain with excellence, and make people feel like they are the only person important in this world, thank you for being such a close friend. Bob Davis who is a master at the Quality Conversation and takes people to the limits of their ability with a smile and determination. Working with you and for you keeps me sharp and inspired no matter what assignment you put me on. Wade Roberts my mentor and conscience. I thank you for your honest feedback and helping me over my self-imposed hurdles! Thanks to all of you that have dedicated your life to service and sales who have taught me so much. You are the role models of how it can be done, every day, every time.

Thank you to my wife who stands by me in all of my pursuits - laughing at me, and with me, making life a pleasure.

I thank my kids, (now adults) for helping me to see from a younger perspective. I appreciate the models you have become for others. Your success is already making differences in the world with everyone you touch. In whatever you do be who you are and keep becoming who you will be, with enthusiasm!

"Rich Hand is a motivating, inspiring, and kind individual with a passion to help others to grow in their own lives.

I am honored to have met Rich. He is selfless in his giving and he truly cares about being an impact to the lives of others"

Mike Lyles
Writer, Speaker

"Rich has been on this journey for many years and I am proud to have shared part of it with him. He is genuine to the core and I love his passion for life"

Wade Roberts
Founder WRC4 Group

"Rich is living what he preaches: a determined life!"

Mike Perkins
Sales Executive

"Rich connects immediately with every audience no matter what size group he speaks to."

Fiona Henderson
VP Events

The  of Satisfaction

Preface

The heartbeat of satisfaction is our ability as individuals to make emotional connections with others. As human beings and customers, all we really want from the people we do business with or have relationships is to be heard, acknowledged and a genuine effort made to solve whatever the issue is. It is really that simple. But every day, every hour, and every minute we know someone has just had a bad experience with a company or person that could have been avoided.

In the customer experience and sales disciplines, we hear stories every day how a person or company doesn't care about their customers. The simple fix is to hire people that genuinely care about people. Can the customer experience ever be perfect? Probably not. But if we try and we try, and we try, and we try we may give some, satisfaction! It takes each and every one of us to work at it every day. If we make better connections with people we will be more effective at the mission of creating a great customer experience. It all revolves around making an emotional connection.

"I Can't Get No Satisfaction!" Famous chorus of a Rolling Stones song titled, "Satisfaction." "I try, and I try, and I try, but I can't get no ♡ satisfaction, no, no, no, hey, hey, hey, that's what I say…" It sometimes feels that way when we are trying to work with some people and organizations these days.

In our personal lives, making emotional connections is the foundation of leaving a positive legacy. Let me share with you how the simple act of volunteering, giving some of my time, became a life changer for me.

The year was 2010 and I was at the bedside of a man that had met Babe Ruth. He was dying but he was still living. He impacted my life in a profound way. My experience as a hospice volunteer changed my life because it made me realize that life was about making connections with people. In the end, nothing else really matters.

As a "companion visit" volunteer for Hospice, my role was to sit with patients that were dying and offer respite for family members that needed a break from watching their loved one. I didn't know this at the time but I was to receive a great gift through my volunteering. There is no greater gift than to be shown what truly matters at the end of life. We often hear people say things like, "life is short, make the best of it", "time goes by in the blink of an eye", but when you are bedside with someone that knows they are dying, and they share with you their deepest feelings about the life they led, you can't let that gift go without thanks. I am so thankful that I have been around people that knew they were dying. Nothing puts life into perspective more than

The  of Satisfaction

dying.

I learned that life and time are precious. I learned to assess what I loved to do and to make time so I could do more of it. I really began to understand that we all have a purpose in life, whether that life is long or short. We are all inter-connected and the things we do impact others in ways we don't always get to see. I learned that I had a greater purpose, and that all of my writing was going to someday have an impact on someone. Sometimes a brief interaction with someone can be a life changing or life-saving event. By making the smallest effort to connect and be kind to people, we can change the course of events.

Hospice volunteering changed the course of my life. The brief connections I made resulted in a more determined me. A more compassionate me. A better me.

I hope my legacy is to have helped others realize their passions. The idea behind the book is to try to emphasize the value of making heartfelt connections with others. I refer to them as emotional connections. The title of the book is "The Heart of Satisfaction; The Power of the Emotional Connection in Sales, Service & Life!" No matter what we do in life, making heartfelt connections with others reaps special rewards for the people that put themselves out there and attempt to make those connections. Whether that is in life or our career, it can make a huge difference in our life in so many ways.

The answer to our life's purpose is in our heart. It is also in the things we choose to do. The time is now to unleash your purpose and start making emotional connections with others. In the end, it is all that will matter. That I have learned from Hospice.

Irwin, a man in his 90's, had very interesting stories to share. Irwin and I both grew up in the Bronx, and could relate to the experiences he had in his youth. I never met Babe Ruth of course, but I had been to the old Yankee Stadium. You can tell what a person values through the stories they tell. He spoke about meeting Babe Ruth. He spoke about taking the train from the Bronx down to 125th street to watch Ben E King and Ella Fitzgerald at the Apollo Theater.

He said his friends thought he was crazy but he loved music and people, all kinds of people. He told stories about how welcomed he felt at the theater, and "Oh the music!" The music was their connection.

He was worried about how emotional his daughters were over his dying. He knew he had lived a full life and he was ready. I felt a great relief to know how resolved someone can be even when knowing death is at the door.

The  of Satisfaction

My wife has worked as a hospice nurse for years and is currently the Executive Director at Gateway House of Peace, where they provide a few beds for hospice patients at no cost. The house is funded totally by the generous gifts of people that support the mission. The founder is a wonderful woman, Joni Hanchett, who decided this was her calling and has provided such a compassionate place for people who are dying and their families to share time together without the worry of finances.

The connections that are built and the amazing things we create when we are determined to act, become the blessings that others treasure. There are opportunities for all of us to find that calling, to share ourselves, and connect with others around us.

I will do my best in these pages to share the reasons I believe making these heartfelt connections are important and the simple things we can do to make those connections. Having spent most of my life in sales and service, I know that making these heartfelt connections can lead to success in everything we do.

Thank you for reading this book. If you like it and find it valuable, please share it with a friend or recommend it to a friend. That would be a wonderful gift; to reach as many people as I can to convince them that the power of genuine, heartfelt connections will make the journey of life more pleasurable and successful.

The  of Satisfaction

Introduction

Making emotional connections is the foundation for a successful career and life. It is particularly important in the sales and customer service industries. Emotional connections are about caring and being selfless in our interactions with others. It is the art of putting others first to help them achieve the things they are interested in. In my career that has spanned beyond 30 years at this point, I have witnessed many people that have a natural ability to connect with others. I have also seen many more that don't seem to have that natural ability and struggle to connect with others. It has interested me throughout my career if this natural ability to connect with people can be taught? Or is connecting and caring something that is built into our DNA? I believe if we make people aware of the things that drive stronger connections they may find making connections a bit easier. This book is an attempt to discuss what we can do as individuals to become more effective at making emotional connections and understand why they are important.

I have had the privilege to spend my career dedicated to serving others. I never tire of it. Actually, I thrive on the energy I get when I have the opportunity to serve. No, I am not senile, yet.

If you have spent your career in retail, restaurants,

sales, or any type of service, you probably have either learned the importance of caring or you naturally care about people.

When you have the opportunity to help people does it feel like adrenalin? Do you find helping others exhilarating in a way that overwhelms any fatigue you may have been feeling? If you find serving people exhilarating - you are destined to be successful in a sales or service career. If you are just starting out, you should pay close attention to how you feel when you have to help people. Do you enjoy it or resent it? If you enjoy it you should consider a career in sales or service.

There are many ways to serve in this life but if you have an interest in making a good living by serving others, you should be aware of how and why emotional connections work. I will provide the information you need to achieve your goals.

Let me share a personal story with you. I have been successful beyond my wildest dreams. I was born the oldest of six. Two of my siblings have mental handicaps. When some people look at them and their lives, they feel sadness. What I can tell you is they are not only happy; they have created a legacy of impacting so many people's lives in a positive way. They have definitely shaped my life in a way that I can only now appreciate as an adult looking back on my life. Their influence has helped me create a career and lifestyle

The  of Satisfaction

that has helped me appreciate how much I have achieved in my life. So much more than I ever imagined. But more importantly, their influence has been instrumental in my pursuit of helping others. I am driven to appreciate people for who they are, why they are special, and making them feel good about who they are.

My purpose for writing this book is to try to help others see the power of making an effort to connect with people, all of the time. I will share how I have mastered certain behaviors and how they impact others. I will explain what behaviors I utilize that help to make better connections with people. I will share stories and examples of making heartfelt connections and how they bring wealth and success to our careers and life. I know that if you make more emotional connections it will be helpful in your pursuit of a fulfilling and purposeful life.

Every day I am so grateful for who I am becoming, the people in my life, and the opportunities I have had because I have mastered the emotional connection. I think everyone can master making genuine heartfelt connections, but I also know many will not know how to do it in a business setting when dealing with customers. You may stumble across bits and pieces of making connections through each of your individual interactions, but I hope this book lays it out for you so you can utilize these connections earlier in your life and career. Additionally, I hope you will enjoy life with a new perspective.

Let's begin the journey.

If we look at the emotional connection as a point within the center of concentric circles, we can see that in order to get to the center we need to penetrate each outer circle.

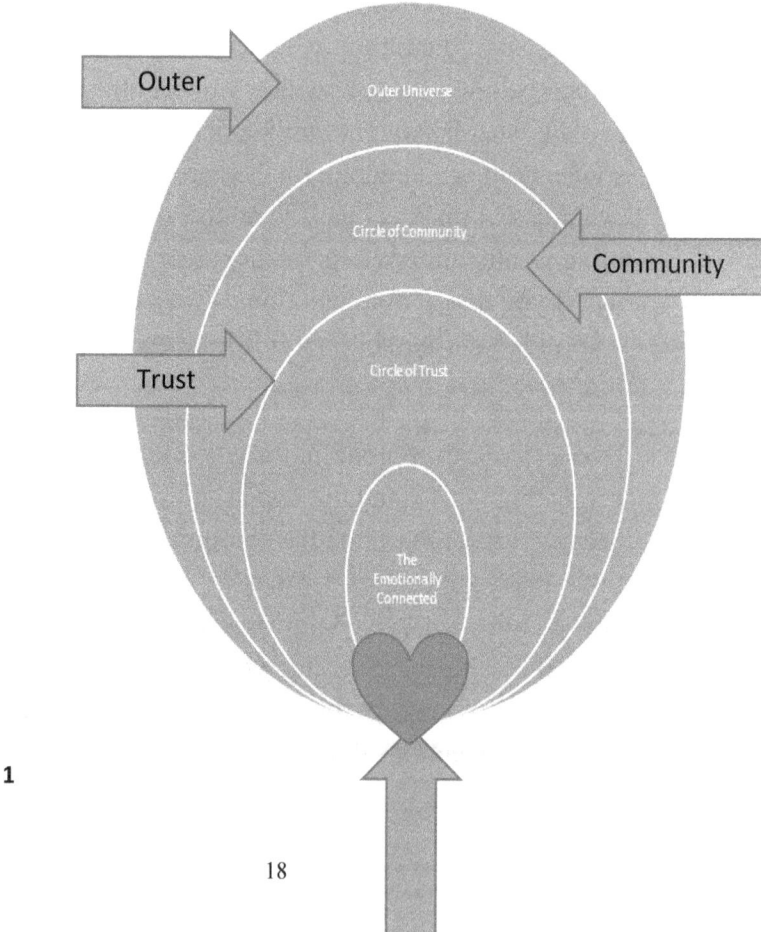

Figure 1

The  of Satisfaction

Getting to the emotional connection is a process. Each connection moves us closer to the inner circle. This process can happen on a 15 minute sales call, a 20 minute service call, or over a long term relationship with a customer. It can also happen in a minute with certain people. The speed of the connection is directly related to the effort and willingness of us to be genuinely interested the people we meet and work with.

Let's look at each of these circles using examples to define each circle within a sales, service, and personal relationship.

The Outer Universe

The outer universe represents people we don't know yet. In the world of personal relationships you have never talked to them, have no known relationship, or known common interests. They represent all of the potential relationships available to you as a person. From the business perspective, these people represent an untapped market for the product or service that you sell. In the marketing world they may represent a list purchase but there is no known relationship at all to the company, product, or service.

Circle of Community

The circle of community represents the people we have something in common with. It may be that we have a common interest and belong to a group or association together. It may be that we have common interests like a sports team, activity such as running or playing an instrument, but the relationship is not personal. There has been no introduction or connection made that has any resemblance of a bond. From the business perspective these are the people that are familiar with your product or service. They may have read an article, visited your website, or inquired about your product or service in some superficial manner.

Circle of Trust

These are people we have met. We have common interests and know each other on the level of sharing a social network relationship, been introduced by a common friend or family member. This group of people is the easiest group of people to make an emotional connection with. From a business perspective they are your customer. They have used your product or service and are familiar with your organization.

The Emotionally Connected

This group is best described as family. Not just family we share DNA with, but people we have developed close and lasting relationships with. This group has a

The  of Satisfaction

bond of trust based on past experiences that have been shared and often are communicated through storytelling. This group gets together at personal functions and whether it is on a regular basis or once a year, once in five years, the bond is deep and strong. It is the people that fit into the category of, "we haven't seen each other in twenty years but we picked right up from where we left off. It's like time never passed for us." Let me share a personal story to illustrate how we move through the circles.

In 1982 my good friend Leif and I were heading off to the same college, SUNY Binghamton. This particular weekend in August we were attending a welcome weekend for transfer students. The mission of the weekend was to get our schedules, learn the ins and outs of the system, and find a place to live. A typical orientation weekend.

We drove the three hours it would take and we arrived on campus with much excitement and enthusiasm that you have when you are embarking on a new adventure. The school put us up for the weekend in one of the dorms and we met a lot of interesting people. We knew we wanted to live off campus so the main mission we were on was to find an apartment off campus.

We did some research and found out there was an off campus housing office at the school with a bulletin board with apartment listings. This was pre-internet where you actually had to search for things by connecting with people, making phone calls, and making appointments to see places in person.

Leif and I showed up at the office and were reviewing the listings. As we were looking for our dream apartment that couldn't be more than $125.00 a month, three other guys showed up and were looking as well. We had no relationship with them. Prior to this meeting they were in the Outer Circle. Since we were now at the same school, looking for an apartment, we quickly moved into the Circle of Community. We started talking and found a number of common interests. Leif and I played guitar and so did Pete, one of the 3 guys at the board. We were all looking for an apartment, and we were all transfers to the school.

We ended up getting an apartment together and began moving into the Circle of Trust. We spent a lot of time together as roommates do. Over the years we have become family. We have attended weddings, child rearing, and funerals. Our connections are deep and emotional. We are emotionally connected. It started with a few questions at a bulletin board: "Are you guys looking for an apartment?", "Where are you from?", "What are you studying?", "What do you like to do?" It ended up with us making connections with these "guys", and it turned out to be life-long relationships with family.

The  of Satisfaction

From a business perspective these are your best customers. These are the customers that you speak to on a regular basis, utilize to introduce new products or services, ask for testimonials, and even if there is a problem with your product or service - the bond is strong enough to maintain them as a customer as long as they believe you are working in their best interest. They are the people that are your greatest marketing resource due to their trust in you and your organization.

These are the definitions of each circle. I used the circles as a way to illustrate the path to making heartfelt emotional connections. When you look at the circles, the idea is that there is a path to the inner circle of the emotionally connected. But the path is not always linear. The path is not always permanent. The groups of individuals and organizations that represent your current emotionally connected individuals/customers may not be the same group today as it will be tomorrow. It is a moving target based on the interactions with your organization and your people.

The focus should always be to retain the current emotional connections you have while increasing the number of people in the inner circle. The only way to do that as an organization is to hire people that know how to make a genuine connection with people in all of the circles.

In our personal relationships the group of emotionally connected individuals is often more permanent than the relationships developed through business connections. For example, it is only in extreme cases that a family member would ever be outside the inner most circle. The bonds of family are much too strong. This is also the case with lifelong friendships that have been developed over many years. In business relationships though, it is much more common and easier to lose someone from the inner circle. In business unlike family, the best way to keep customers in your inner circle is to nurture that relationship with emotional connections on a regular basis with consistency, in every interaction with your customer. The consistency is critical when we are talking about sales and service organizations.

So the question becomes: why is it important to move people and customers into the most inner circle of the emotionally connected?

In your personal life it means better relationships and a happier life. In sales it means more customers, more committed customers, more sales, more profitable sales, more revenue, and more money for you as a sales person. In customer service it means retaining more customers, improving profitability for the company, increasing revenue and potential revenue, building a fan

The  of Satisfaction

base for your organization, and it increases your value to the organization. In addition it builds a rewarding career and improves your outlook for promotions and a better life.

If this is true, the next question is: why do emotional connections result in all of this success?

Before we can answer this question we must understand what behaviors lead to emotional connections. Once we have determined the behaviors and how people react to them, we can understand the absolute power emotional connections have in determining an individual's and organization's success.

The Behaviors That Lead to Emotional Connections

Empathy

You often hear people in sales and service throw around the word empathy. But what is empathy? The textbook definition is simply: "the ability to put yourself in someone else's situation." That sounds very simple but what does it mean in real life?

I mentioned earlier I grew up in a family of six. I was the oldest of three boys and three girls. My sister Eugenia (Gena) was born two years after me and was mentally handicapped. Gena is a high functioning individual who understands much of what goes on around her but at an 8-10 year old perspective. Her blessing is her truthfulness, and her curse is her truthfulness. If you want to keep something secret you keep it from Gena.

Philip is my youngest brother born 5th in the lineup. Philip cannot speak much but he understands at a very complex level. He understands when people are mad at each other, happy with each other, need attention, but cannot understand how to tie a pair of shoes. I have always believed that is because he is smart enough to know if you act like you can't do something, someone else will do it for you. He would be a great husband with this characteristic.

The  of Satisfaction

Gena and Philip have shaped my life in ways I could spend an entire book on, but the greatest gift they have given me is the ability to empathize. The many challenges of growing up caring for and protecting my brother and sister have made me highly sensitive to other people's feelings and the value of those feelings. I am prone to help the people that need the most help. I find myself going beyond the norm to include people in a group or conversation knowing how it feels to be excluded because you are different or shy, or handicapped in some way.

This quality of being able to empathize is a "skill" that is critical to building emotional connections and people skills. The genuine interest in understanding where people are coming from lays a foundation for building skills like conversation, networking, facilitation, analytical, situational awareness, presentation, and a host of other skills proven to be necessary for a successful life in sales or service.

The role of empathy in situations is critical, although critical seems to be the wrong word. The right word is foundational to building an emotional connection. If you think about anyone you have a strong connection with, you will quickly conclude the reason is that you care about that person deeply. You honestly and genuinely care what happens to that person and when you are in a conversation with them you want to understand and help them if the opportunity arises.

If you don't have empathy in your heart, you are lacking the ability to genuinely care about that person.

How can you build an emotional connection if you don't care? How can you care about someone you just met? Why should you care about someone you just met?

The ability to connect with people that you don't care about can be perceived as phony if you truly don't care about them. It is impossible to hide a lack of empathy for others. Whether that is a sale, an attempt to retain a customer, or to simply influence another person. For example, when you are buying something from someone and they tell you they like your dress but you know they don't give a darn about your dress, they just want to sell you the Lexus. I will expand further on this but to sell without empathy is to be a sales person just going through the motions, and you are simply doing "transactional" sales. These are the least rewarding sales because it is about the process not the person.

These are the sales that create the greatest "buyer's remorse." These are often the sales that never come to fruition and the customer backs out prior to instillation returns your product, or cancels the service call. They also will not be a supporter of your product or service and will actually tell friends and colleagues to avoid your organization.

The  of Satisfaction

Most people have been trained in sales and customer service to follow a process flow. Most sales people have been trained that sales is a numbers "game" and in some ways it is. But if you want to have a rewarding and successful career in sales or service, it is not a "game" to be played but a relationship to be built. Even if that relationship is ten minutes or an hour, an empathetic person can make the impression last a lifetime. Think about your best experiences buying something in your life. You probably remember how that sales person made you feel about the experience. You probably don't remember the transaction details but I expect you remember the feeling you left with after purchasing that product.

Let me share another personal story to emphasize empathy. When my wife and I bought our first house we didn't understand the process. So one day we just set out to look at houses to see what was out there. We didn't have a Realtor and just called the phone number on the sign in front of the house. We had encounters with three agents until we met Charlie. The first three agents had only one thing in mind; a sale. Not one of the three cared enough to ask us the questions that we eventually were asked by Charlie. Charlie spent his time asking about me and my wife. He asked about our goals, were we planning a family, what were our financial goals. He didn't even seem to want to sell us a house. He seemed like he was someone you meet at a party, and become immediate friends. We bought our first house from Charlie. What Charlie understood was in sales it is about building trust and understanding the customer. He made an emotional connection with me and my wife!

In customer service you are taught to put yourself in the customer's shoes. You often find yourself in a position where you may have to provide information the customer may not be happy about. This is where the ability to create an emotional connection quickly, and provide a solution that puts the customer in the driver's seat, by giving them choices, is priceless to an organization. The ability to take on bad news with confidence, using the right pitch, tone, and word choice is just the foundation. If you can create that genuine connection with the customer, they are more likely to remember the experience in a much better light. If they are then given choices and feel they were given the ability to be part of the solution, they are likely to become a loyal customer based on the experience.

I have been a loyal customer for a number of services we use. My wife and I were willing to pay more for our insurance because we trusted our agent to protect our assets and update our coverage when it was necessary. We had a significant amount of damage to our home from a hail storm and the assessor would not cover an

The  of Satisfaction

item we thought should have been. Our agent could not change the decision but he gave us a few options in our coverage that saved a few dollars and we accepted the decision. If it was not for him, we would have switched companies. That would have meant thousands of dollars of lost premiums for the company.

We had an emotional connection with the agent, not the company. Lucky for that company. I believe this is a key point to understand. Customers see the people they deal with on the phone, through e-mail, or inside the store as the company. And if the company does something not controlled by that agent or salesperson, an emotional connection can be the difference between keeping and losing the customer. We remained a customer for thirteen years because of the agent, not particularly the company, until we moved from the state!

So how do you care about someone you just met? In our daily lives we meet many people for a brief moment and sometimes we walk away from that moment with a sense of making an emotional connection with that person. Then there are times we meet someone for a brief moment and there is no connection. The difference is simply that when we extend genuine empathy toward an individual we feel a connection. Often when we extend an empathetic moment the individual responds with a smile or a kind word. But the kind word is not the driver here – it is our effort that makes us feel connected, therefore forming an emotional connection.

The ability to make emotional connections starts with US/WE/YOU making an effort to empathize with the individual. Have you ever helped an older person lift a heavy package, mow their lawn, or grabbed their bag from the overhead bin in an airplane? Why did you do it? Did they ask you to do it or did you put yourself in their shoes and take initiative to help them? If the answer is you initiated the activity then you more than likely created a connected moment with that individual.

So why do we want to make emotional connections? The first and most simple answer is it feels good for us. It may sound selfish but I believe we can't be selfless without a bit of selfishness. It feels good to help others. It makes us better people when we help others. We become better at what we do in our lives when we help others. So there is a small component of selfishness but for the right reasons.

In sales and service the people that know how to connect with people are always a top performer in the organization, and often get promoted because they have great "people" skills. It is simply that they put others first to help them get what they need, and in turn reap the rewards.

The  of Satisfaction

If we look back at Figure 1 again and apply empathy to the concentric circles, what opportunities do we see to increase the number of individuals in the inner circle? Why do we want to increase the inner circles?

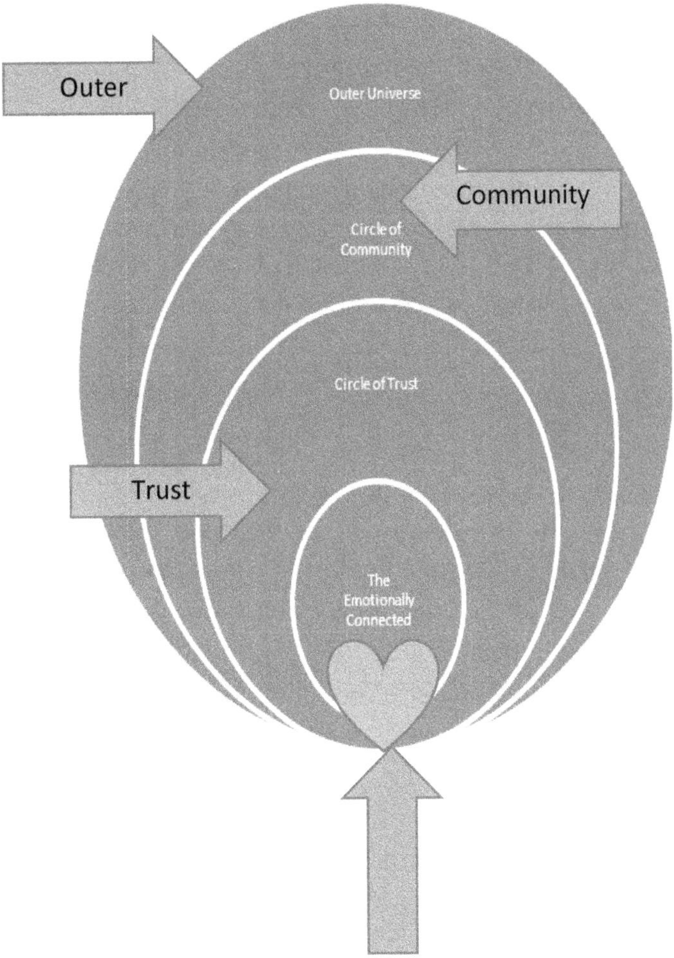

Figure 1

If we start with the foundational characteristic of empathy, and since we know connections can be made in short time frames, if we initiate the emotional connection, we can move people from the "Outer Universe" to the "Circle of Community" very quickly. The emotional connections we make give us the opportunity to move more people into the "Circle of Trust" which is where we need people to be to create lasting relationships.

In real life that means a larger and more connected circle of friends. In sales and service it means more sales, better retention of customers, and the greater possibility of positive organic growth through word of mouth for you or your organization.

Initiate the Connection

If making an emotional connection depends on our actions, does it make sense that we can improve the number of connections we make? If it doesn't depend on anyone else initiating the connection, the only limit we have to grow our spheres of influence is our effort to do so.

Many people believe that they can't make a connection with someone if the person they are trying to connect with doesn't respond to the signals, and that is partly true. But the response of people to your efforts is most

The  of Satisfaction

often dependent on our initial approach to the relationship or situation.

Unfortunately, for too long, people have been conditioned to keep strangers at arms-length and treat everyone with suspicion. This conditioning is a survival tactic we teach our children and has merit for that purpose. The initial emotional connection if genuine and sincere can overcome this reflective response in most cases. Sometimes people respond by saying "I didn't expect that!" It is true that emotional connections are the exception, not the rule. But if we utilize our empathy, and genuinely care about others, our efforts will be well worth the satisfaction you will receive by making a heartfelt connection.

Can we teach empathy? I am not sure we can teach it but we can explain it so that everyone can use their own experiences to apply it to make better emotional connections. We all have different experiences that shape our upbringing. The key is to take those experiences and learn how they can be applied to help us learn more about others.

Empathy is the foundational element but as everything in life, it is just one component of a complex set of circumstances that makes each interaction a successful connection. Some of the elements are so simple you will just smile, and others may have you scratching your head. But in the end it is a recipe that needs to be re-created and customized for every individual emotional connection you make.

I thought I would share a memory growing up and let you use your analytical skills to decide how this memory impacted my desire to make emotional connections. The setting is a crowded restaurant with dozens of tables, creating an almost circular, dynamic circus environment. The restaurant was loud with families eating their meals, laughing and doing what families did at dinner in the 70's. In today's world no one may have noticed our family because their heads would be in their personal device. Just an observation not a judgement but I digress.

The fact that our family rarely went out to dinner, and when we did we needed a table for eight, it just so happened that big tables always seemed to be in the middle of the restaurant. Even in the least dysfunctional families, the entry into a restaurant to sit at the center table can be a spectacle. It often included my brother and sister wanting to sit next to each other or apart. It was a jockeying for position and sometimes a play for the few coloring books and crayons that were put on the table for entertainment (Remember this is the 70's). But it rarely was a smooth, quiet, or orderly process when the oldest of six children is 12 and the youngest 2.

As we were entering, the usual turning of the heads by

The  of Satisfaction

nearby tables was occurring to no surprise. But as was often the case, two of my non handicapped siblings started fighting over seats. This escalated into a scene where mom and dad had to intervene which then set off Gena into an uncontrollable need to get involved in a very loud voice. As my mother now turned her attention to Gena from the fighting siblings, Phil butted in to diplomatically control the situation with some grunts and physical activity. We had a regular circus going on in the center ring. Still not abnormal at this point. But Gena continued to loudly express her disappointment with her siblings and how my mother was not controlling them when at the table next to us I overheard a couple. Their words scarred me. "It is so sad that they have a mentally retarded daughter and I think there is something wrong with the boy (I assume looking at Phil but it could have been me). But when I heard "I don't know why people keep children like that and don't put them in an institution…" my life changed. I wanted to tell them how much joy Gena and Philip brought to our family. It made me very angry that people could make such superficial judgements without knowing the circumstances and not knowing Gena and Phil. The thing I knew was that Gena and Philip added more love to this world than many "normal" people ever could!

I spent many years working for my Mother's Day Camp, "Camp Venture: A Place in the Sun" in the summer. It was a camp that was a respite for the mentally and physically handicapped, and a safe place from ridicule just to be kids for a summer. Everyone is brought into this life for a purpose. I now know why Gena and Phil are my brother and sister. I would not be who I am today without them; period. This experience at Camp Venture gave me a deep respect for every human being. We helped the most handicapped individuals have just a bit of joy in a life that was heartbreaking when you thought about it too hard. I have never felt more joy than when I was helping kids at Camp Venture.

I believe everyone has examples in their lives of people and situations that have made a deep impact emotionally, and these situations play a role in who we become as adults. Helping people connect with the stories of their life experiences can help us to help them understand the power of empathy. The ability to understand empathy and how it drives us is key to making deep and lasting connections.

Let's look at other behaviors that impact the ability to make an emotional connection.

Timing

We may not think about timing when we think about making emotional connections, but similar to delivering a punch line in comedy, an emotional connection works in a similar way. If you don't time your connection

The  of Satisfaction

correctly it can be misconstrued by the individual you are trying to connect with. Jerry Seinfeld is a comedic genius in his delivery. Ellen DeGeneres is a comedic genius. Oprah is a TV talk show genius. Hugh Hewitt is a talk radio genius.

What each of these professionals have in common is their understanding of how timing impacts their craft. They all have other characteristics and skills that round out their genius in their field but if you watch and listen to them in comparison to their peers they excel at the art of timing and making connections with their audience.

Our ability to connect with people is impacted by timing in a number of practical ways. For example, if you are talking to a prospect on the phone and they just communicated they had a death in the family, it is not the appropriate time to talk about your product or service. It is time to acknowledge the loss that the customer just shared with you. For example, a customer calls your organization and they share that their spouse recently passed and they were calling to make a change to their service with your organization. The appropriate response might sound like this: *"Thank you so much for calling today. I am so sorry to hear about your spouse. I am sure this is a difficult time for you and I am here to help you make any adjustments to your account you need. I know this may become difficult for you and I will do my best to make this as easy as I can for you."* If you or your team is not connecting with your customers at this level, you have an opportunity to improve the service at your organization or the service you provide.

You need to know when to approach a subject with an individual. In the same manner Oprah approaches a guest on her program that has experienced a tragedy is an example of understanding the power of emotional connections. Her facial expressions, inflection in her voice, her body language, the questions she chooses to ask, and her overall demeanor, "hug" the person being interviewed. The audience becomes completely engulfed in her interview and feel they are the only people in the room with Oprah.

When Oprah asks a question, she listens to the response of the guest, and with impeccable timing, asks the next question in a way that is therapeutic to both the interviewee and the audience. People wait on the edge of their seats not only for the answers but the response and next question from Oprah. She is a master at the emotional connection because you can tell she genuinely cares about the people she interacts with. It is why she is the success she is and continues to be in the world of talk shows.

If an interview by Oprah moves you, then you understand the power of the emotional connection.

The  of Satisfaction

When you understand how she does it, you will command the ability to make the emotional connection.

Active Listening

Have you ever been in a social setting and start talking with someone you just met, and the person keeps breaking eye contact to look around the room while you're talking? How does that make you feel? When we choose to engage with people, no matter who, why, where or when, we must give that person our undivided attention if we want to make an emotional connection.

It does not matter whether we are on the phone or in person, it is important to let the person we are speaking with know we are listening. In person the most apparent way we know someone is listening is through eye contact. It is also common to nod our heads as if we are saying yes as we look deeply into the person's eyes.

On the phone we need to use verbal cues to let the person know we are listening. We can use the same head nod but that is more to make the verbal cue seem more natural over the phone. I often see agents in call centers leaning back in their chairs when talking to customers on the phone and I will ask them, "do you think the customer can tell how you are sitting in your chair?" They look at me as if I have two heads and say "of course not." Well I will tell you that the sound of your voice directly follows the posture you take with your body.

If you are sitting forward you will seem more engaged to the person on the other end of the phone. If you are standing up, your elevated stature will make you feel more powerful, and therefore sound more confident on the phone.

The method of communication - whether it is over the phone or in person does not matter when it comes to actively listening. We need to ensure we use all of our available senses to communicate. Tone, inflection, verbal cues, body language, and a genuine interest in what the person is saying all come together to set up an opportunity to make an emotional connection.

Active listening is simply showing respect and giving the person your undivided attention.

As you think about ways we can actively listen, don't forget the most important part of actively listening, the opportunity to learn about that person!

Asking Relevant Questions

In addition to actively listening and understanding the importance of timing in our interactions, how and what we ask helps us to make a stronger emotional connection. If you are speaking with someone and you mention that today is your birthday, and they don't say Happy Birthday! How do you think you would feel?

The  of Satisfaction

What if that person said Happy Birthday! Enthusiastically, and then asked: "are you doing anything special on this important day?" Do you think that question says anything about the person asking it? If you ask two to three additional questions of that person based on their responses to each question and listen closely you will more than likely learn something interesting about that person.

When we ask questions of the people we meet that are relevant and personal, we create an emotional connection. It opens up a dialogue that can continue to flow deeper into a conversation that has meaning. It is not just a space filler question like "How's the weather?" Questions like *"How's the weather?"* are often interpreted, not as a question that shows caring, but rather a lack of effort to engage in a more connecting conversation. That is unless there is a significant weather event that has recently happened in their area. For example, *"I see you're from Oklahoma, are you near where the recent tornado touched down?"* If you are asking a weather question, make it specific.

Timing, actively listening, and asking relevant questions can all be used to build closer personal relationships, and help you to be better at customer service or sales. When we talk about moving our relationships/customers from the Circle of Community to the Circle of Trust, it is important to think about how these powerful steps in the interaction when applied work.

When we talk with our customers and are committed to making emotional connections it is important to practice. Try to put yourself in the other person's shoes and grade your conversation honestly on the basis of building a strong connection with the other person. By being self-aware in how we are being received in our communication with others is critical. The next time you are speaking with a friend or customer, think about the questions you ask in the conversation. Make sure you ask at least 3 questions that are focused on the other person. Make sure the questions are relevant to the conversation and be aware of the timing and delivery. Ask questions based on the responses of the other person that are personal and important to that person. For example, if you are taking an order for flowers over the phone start by asking, *"Is this a special occasion?"* or *"This is for your anniversary, well Happy Anniversary!, how many years have you and your spouse been married?"*

By being more aware of how you are connecting with the other person you will begin to realize how these additional questions start impacting the number of genuine connections you make. This will in turn impact your effectiveness at sales and or service.

The  of Satisfaction

Honesty

Honesty is the best policy in life. There are no exceptions. In sales and service, many sales people believe they have to manipulate the conversation to "win" a sale or "save" an account. This is wrong. We never manipulate. We position the issue with the information necessary for our customer to make a good decision for them. You can't make an emotional connection without being honest. Emotional connections can only be developed on trust. You can't trust people that are not honest. If we look at figure 1 again, it is called the Circle of Trust. To get to an emotional connection, you have to pass through The Circle of Trust. No honesty, no trust, no connection.

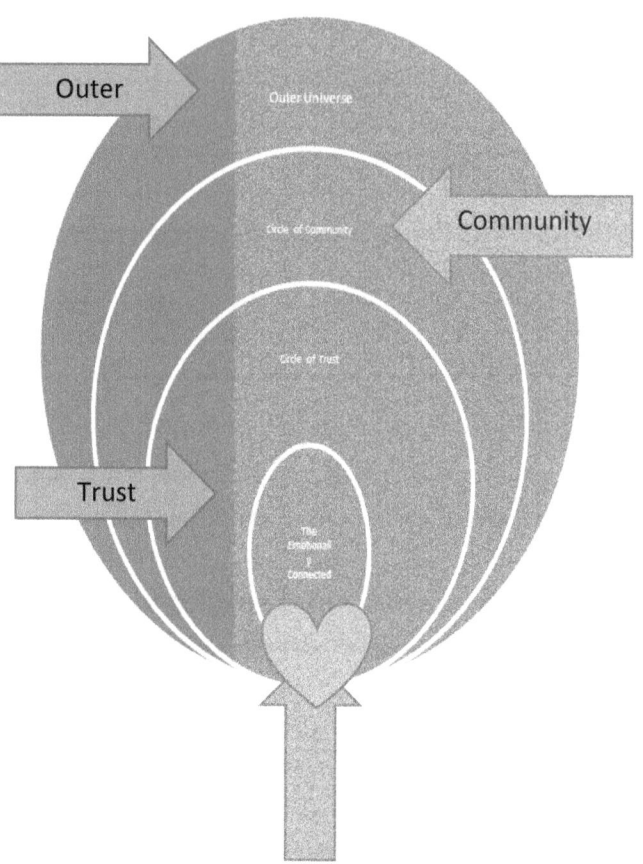

It is not honest to leave out relevant information in a conversation. This is counter intuitive for some sales people. Many sales people think that if they avoid deficiencies in their product or service they are more likely to win the sale. It is actually the opposite. If you leave out relevant information about your product or service, and later in the conversation or relationship the

The  of Satisfaction

question is raised, and now you must reveal the deficiency, you have just flushed all of the trust you may have built over time in one brief moment. The customer will now know you knew information that was important to them but you chose to keep it from them. They now know you are looking out for you, not them.

The way we approach an issue and the words we use makes all the difference in making the connection. By working through the deficiency transparently and honestly, the trust is built. If the customer is assured you are looking out for them by bringing it to their attention, they are likely to minimize and justify a work around if they believe the final outcome will be good for them. There will be times when what you sell is not right for a customer, and by steering them in the right direction which may not include your product, they will recommend you or your organization to others. If circumstances change in the future, they will become a customer at some point and may send other customers to you in the meantime. But only if they trust you and know you have their best interest in mind.

The best approach is to make sure you ask enough relevant questions to understand the customer's issue so you can position your response in a positive manner. If a customer is interested in a feature and your product is known to have issues with this particular component, learn all you can about the customer's interest and understanding of that feature. You may find that what they perceived, and what is reality about this feature can be addressed by another part of your product's solution. The more you know about the customer's needs, the more opportunity you will have to build a strong connection with the customer and satisfy their interests. This approach will lay a foundation for building an emotional connection with this customer.

In our personal interactions with people, being honest is the foundation to a lasting connection with that person. If we can't be honest, we can never build an emotional connection because we will never have the foundation necessary to build the relationship.

Sincerity

The definition of being sincere: "Free from pretense or deceit; proceeding from genuine feelings…"

When we want to make an emotional connection, does it make sense that we should make stuff up and be deceitful at the start of the relationship? Of course not. To live a fulfilling life it is important to care about others and treat others the way we want to be treated. If you give me one sincere sales person to your three insincere sales people, I will take the one sales person and be as productive as the other three. When you operate from a position of sincerity you never falter in your commitment to the person you are trying to help,

The  of Satisfaction

sell something to, or develop a relationship with. People that are insincere always show their true feelings at some point and this impacts the relationship negatively, and the numbers in sales or service.

By being sincere we send a message to the world that we truly care. It tells people we are open and willing to listen to them to understand how we can be of service. It also feels good. When we are genuinely sincere, we have the heart necessary to build emotional connections.

Genuine

The definition of being genuine: "To be authentic."

When we are authentic we are who we are. No window dressings to please others. Just the natural state of our being. You can see that authentic and genuine go hand and hand. In the study of human behavior, we see some people are naturally gifted at some of these characteristics but being genuine is a true reflection of our experiences in life and how we apply them to our circumstances, and the circumstances of others.

My state as a human being has been impacted deeply by my childhood experiences. I use these experiences in every interaction with other human beings. I use these experiences to build my situational awareness and apply them to the interaction. It happens in a nano second but it is a very complex process in the brain. Only if we take the time to analyze our interactions and why we chose a certain path of behavior can we understand the power of the emotional connection.

Let's take a simple example that happens every day. You pull into the parking lot of the local convenient store. You exit your car and start heading toward the door. Someone from another vehicle is approaching the door at the same time. This is not one of those automatic doors that open on their own. Our "situational awareness" determines the next behavior. Is it someone open to making a connection? What is their body language? If it is a female (in my case being a male and brought up as a gentleman), am I going to open the door? In my quick scan of her/his behavior is he/she likely to be receptive to that action? Is she elderly? Is he young? Do I make any sort of comment? Should I choose to make an emotional connection? What is my state of being? Should I simply smile? As I open the door should I choose to say a kind word? Is there anything going on around us that I can comment on to make the connection?

I am only scratching the surface here of what is going on in our brain in the seconds leading up to this encounter. The point I want to get across is if we analyze what is happening, we begin to understand how our actions and choices either make or avoid connecting with others. It is truly in our control how this simple

The  of Satisfaction

encounter can become a moment that changes someone's day and even our own day.

We will talk specifically about situational awareness soon. The point being that when we are genuine and authentic we can impact more people in a positive way by being aware of how our backgrounds give us the tools to be a better person. And how we translate that to an emotional connection.

Smile!

Everyone loves a smile! Our smile is a great way to change the attitude in a room, at any social gathering, and over the phone. Our body language translates over the phone and when we smile it comes through loud and clear. Speak with a smile!

As with any human interaction, timing plays a role in when we use a smile and what type of smile we use. Smiles have a type? Yes they do. Think about the last smile you shared with someone. What type of smile was it? Was it a full teeth grin where your cheeks were touching your forehead? Was it a "soft" smile acknowledging a glance from a colleague in a meeting? Was it the smile when you learned you just got a raise? If you think about the act of smiling, there are many components to the act and delivery of a smile.

When we want to make an emotional connection, the

smile can be the easiest entry point to building a stronger relationship. The smile must be sincere, genuine, and come from the heart. A "fake" smile ,like every other form of human deception, can be detected. When was the last time you used a "fake" smile? Fake smiles are generally used to be polite. For example, a new boss that has not taken the time to introduce him/herself to the team but demands everyone stay late for a last minute conference call at work. The fake smile is simply a polite gesture replacing the gesture you would like to make. It is best not to smile at all. Be genuine, honest, and sincere in everything you do.

The smile combined with enthusiasm is contagious. When you walk into a room does it "light up"? The next time you walk into a room try this: think about all of the blessings in your life, your kids, your health, an upcoming family vacation, and smile ear to ear. Then with enthusiasm say hello to everyone in the room and say, *"it's going to be a great day!"* The room will be brighter and the people in it will be happy you just joined them. If you do this when you arrive at work or when you arrive at every meeting, you will find that the setting will be brighter and happier because you arrived. What will begin to happen after a consistent practice of entering a room in this manner is that the people in it will be smiling before you even get the chance to greet them. Every meeting you enter will be conducted in a more enthusiastic atmosphere and you

The  of Satisfaction

will become the person people want in their meeting.

Keep smiling and stay enthusiastic wherever you go and with whomever you meet, and it will seem that everywhere you go people are enthusiastic and happy to be there. It is a much more rewarding and productive way to go through life. It will seem as if you are getting better opportunities at work, selling more, retaining more customers, and the future will seem much brighter. It will seem that way because you are making more heartfelt connections with people. It will seem things are better in your life because things are better in your life.

Inflection

Inflection is the art of using the tone of your voice, speed, volume all in synchronicity to connect with another's emotion. Inflection is a natural part of showing empathy for others. The use of inflection makes any interaction with our customers more effective. It is especially important in the call center world where customers perceive call center agents to be scripted. If people believe you are scripted, all credibility is lost. Scripting agents on the phone is a lot easier than training them to make real and genuine connections. But there is a cost to scripting. The cost is the customer's perception that an agent cares.

It is important to understand inflection but difficult to describe in writing. Saying words softly show sensitivity. Slightly increased volume and steady tones are received as confidence. When reading any material to our customers we should change speed, volume, and use an occasional pause to make listening more interesting to the other person when done effectively. Using inflection makes us more human. Making ourselves more human is what we want to do when dealing with others.

Situational Awareness

I mentioned situational awareness earlier. Situational awareness is a really important part of making connections with others. Let's start by defining the term.

Situational Awareness: "The ability of an individual to immediately understand the circumstances surrounding them."

It is similar to what some people call a "sixth sense." People with a sixth sense have the ability to almost predict the immediate future. I believe this is simply hyper situational awareness. Let me try and explain what I mean. You walk into a convenient store while making a stop to get gas. The store is crowded and as you walk through the door you see three people that look like they are about to rob the store. How would you know that? What is it about the situation that

The  of Satisfaction

indicates the people are about to rob the store?

The three people you scanned most likely had a look on their faces that immediately raised your suspicion. What indicates a suspicious look? Did these people have a look in their eyes? Did they not make eye contact? Was their body language anxious and uncomfortable?

As you scanned and noticed one person that looked "suspicious", this prompted you to look at others in the store with a similar posture, look, or familiar stance and you immediately connected three potential people with similar traits. Maybe they had similar clothing and each of their sides was bulging with something under their shirt that could be a weapon.

If you were to set up a scenario as I have above, and had 100 people walk in that store as an experiment to see if they had any situational awareness skills, depending on how obvious you made the three characters look, a majority of people would simply go into the store, get their coffee, and notice nothing unusual. Some people would not notice the scenario even if the three characters were holding weapons and standing by the counter when they came in. Some people may not even notice the situation even if the three characters were yelling at the counter asking the store cashier for their money.

This scenario is familiar to people who have watched programs like CSI, Blue Bloods, and many other law enforcement shows. In a sales encounter or a service exchange, situational awareness is a critical skill.

In the contact center all you have is a voice on the other end of the phone to determine the situation. Whether you are selling over the phone or providing customer service, understanding the situation is critical for improving the ability to provide an excellent outcome. So how do you use situational awareness to make the exchange go the way you want it to go?

Let's take the example of a customer calling in to a call center to purchase a product. The moment the agent ends their greeting the agent must calculate multiple inputs at once. They must calculate the tone of the voice to understand if the customer is smiling, indifferent, or angry. The agent must listen to the speed of the customer's words, and the volume. The agent should be listening to any background noise that can help determine the customer's situation. And of course the content of the opening sentence to determine the best response for the situation.

If the agent isn't actively listening from the second that customer starts speaking it could mean the difference between an excellent customer experience or sale and a poor experience or the loss of a sale.

The  of Satisfaction

Let's look at an example:

Me: "Thank you for calling Hand Written Productions, my name is Rich, how may I assist you today?" (said with enthusiasm)

Customer: "Yes hello (said slightly distracted), I would like to (pause) yes I would like to know (car noise in background) where I can buy your book?"

In this scenario there are a few things to key in on. The caller is distracted. We know this because we can hear it in their voice through a pause, and the fact they repeat themselves after the pause. We also know they are driving which can impact the amount of time you have with the customer, and the customer's ability to listen closely to details. We will want to acknowledge the customer's situation with statements and clarifying questions to be most effective.

Me: "I can absolutely help you to find a place to buy my book, who do I have the pleasure of speaking with today?"

Customer: "Joe"

Me: "Thanks Joe, it sounds like you are driving so I will make this as quick as possible. Do you normally buy your books online or at a retail location?"

Customer: "Yes thank you, I am driving so I can't write

anything down and I'm almost to work. I only have a few minutes to talk..."

In the example, we listen to understand the situation, and adjusted our response to determine the best way to approach the call. It is a very simple illustration but all too often agents miss these queues from the customer. Do you think the response and questions were effective? Did this example help explain what I mean by situational awareness? Would you have done it the same or different?

When we deal with customers in person it is a bit easier because you have visual clues to help determine the customer's situation. The customer may be confused or distracted by children, but you use the same method to connect. You use the situational awareness to determine your responses to the customer. There are so many clues that people share and so many of us don't utilize our senses to make a better connection with our customers.

By being aware of everything around us, we can make better connections with our customers. Next time a customer comes in your store when it is raining outside, use the circumstance to spark up a conversation and make a connection. The customer will appreciate it and more than likely stay in your store just a bit longer, and maybe even purchase more!

The  of Satisfaction

Becoming an Emotional Connector

What is an Emotional Connector? An Emotional Connector (EC) is a person that exemplifies all of the traits we have been talking about throughout the book. My definition is: *"Someone that is enthusiastic, has a constant smile, deliberately makes the effort to connect with people, is genuinely interested in helping people, and does it every day."*

Have you ever met that person that everyone gravitates to? The person that lights up the room when they walk in? This person is likely an Emotional Connector. When you meet an EC there is no doubt. This is what you need to do to become an Emotional Connector:

- Decide you are going to be an EC and deliberately connect with people.
- Be enthusiastic in everything you do. There is no room for negativity. Be grateful and be thankful every day for what you have, and never dwell on what you don't have.
- Fine tune your situational awareness skills. Be aware of everything going on around you.
- Be empathetic and place yourself in other people's shoes; always.
- Learn about people by asking them questions and refrain from telling. Listen, Listen, Listen.

- Be genuinely interested in people and try to learn more about them.
- Use what you learn about people to help them achieve their goals not yours. Your goal should be to help them.
- Learn from every interaction and continuously improve your skills to become an Emotional Connector.

To become an EC, you simply have to apply what we have been discussing, every day. You will become the person that people want to be around and light up the room.

You can choose to be an EC in your job as a sales person or service representative, or to live a successful life in general.

An important part of being successful at making emotional connections is the ability to understand the type of personality you are dealing with. There are formal methods to learn about personality types, and we can learn through observation.

The  of Satisfaction

Personality Types and Why It Matters in Making Emotional Connections

Whether you are talking to someone in person or on the phone, developing the skill to recognize personality types is critical in creating emotional connections in sales, service and life.

How do we know what type of personality someone has? There are a number of methods to determine personality types and I encourage you to become familiar with them. When you understand how people perceive others, the easier it becomes to make these emotional connections.

When we are dealing with customers, identifying the type of person you are dealing with helps to determine the approach to take to make a connection.

I will describe the main personality types and how these personalities interact in general. For most of us, collaborating as part of a team is common in the work place. As a leader, knowing the dynamics of personality types can help you to become more effective at working within those teams.

Organizations overlook the power of personalities in the success or failures of projects. By understanding these personality types, we can make better connections, therefore becoming more effective.

According to Enterprise Project Management, 70% of all projects fail. That is a disturbing number. There are many reasons projects fail, but one reason is a lack of team work. The best way to determine the most effective team to drive a project to success is understanding how people will work together - or not. I have seen too many projects undermined because of personal conflicts between team members.

There are many ways to build teams. Let's look at a sports analogy. When we look at a successful sports team does each player have the same skills? More specifically, does a pitcher and outfielder have the same skill? Does a quarterback and a cornerback have the same skills? They are both athletic but a pitcher and quarterback have unique skills to be successful at their position. The same is true for the outfielder and cornerback.

To build a successful team, a coach/leader knows that each position has a specific and unique role in the success of the team. You would never build a sport's team with all pitchers or quarterbacks, would you? How successful can a team be if everyone comes to the table

The  of Satisfaction

with the same skill?

In business and in most ventures in life, a diverse skill set is critical to the success of any project or venture. Most successful projects are composed of various positions, playing specific and unique roles, often including: a strong project manager, an IT manager, marketing/sales manager, engineer, financial people, and manufacturing or service expertise. Depending on your industry, the roles and positions may have different names, but these are representative of some key players needed to complete a successful business project.

It is true that certain personality types gravitate toward specific roles. This is a generalization and there are always exceptions, but engineers and IT (especially software developers) tend to be introverted, avoid socializing, which makes them likely to hold back valuable information. Because they are not comfortable in groups, and may feel uncomfortable engaging the group, valuable information may be overlooked if the project manager (or others in the group) don't understand how to get them to engage with the group. Financial people tend to be very detailed oriented and have difficulty seeing the bigger picture and more creative visions of a projects scope. They need to "run the numbers" before being convinced to support any group efforts. Sales people tend to see only the bright side of a project and can often be blindsided by details they would rather not see if it means changing a direction in the project.

Again, these are very generic examples, but anyone having spent time on company projects has had the opportunity to observe a lot of teams, and see this dynamic in action. So how successful do you think a project with a team of all sales people would be? If it is a project to decide a new software program for the call center, what would you expect the results to be? It would most likely have many gaps and opportunities because the vision came from "one" position's perspective.

So if we agree that it makes sense to have diverse roles on a team, and those roles attract certain personality types, would it be helpful to understand how these personality types work together? It is critical actually. As we discussed, 70% of projects fail. One reason can be traced to the dynamic of the team. If the members of the team do not understand how to interact with each other, and therefore no longer operate as a team, but rather adversaries, how successful can they be? The team can break down to the point that people are outright undermining the other team members, and the project fails.

So let's understand a few of the personalities.

The  of Satisfaction

Driven, Confident, and Dominating.

This personality type is very confident and can dominate conversations. When confident and dominating personalities on a team interact with other personality types, they tend to limit the conversations and openness of the group, not always intentionally, but rather as a matter of how they can intimidate the humble and more accommodating personalities on the team. Even analytical and systematic people may be cautious to engage, as not to be seen as challenging the dominating personality.

Because driven, confident, and dominating people often are in key leadership positions, they can make sharing ideas in a team environment difficult. Many of this personality type also are challenged with having patience. Confident people tend to discount the humble members of the team. It is imperative to understand; this personality type must be managed by the team leader so they don't overtake the mission of the team.

Analytical and Systematic.

People that are more analytical and systematic need to have details to feel comfortable to make decisions. This personality type can drive the optimistic and outgoing people crazy. When the outgoing optimistic people are chasing the shiny bright objects, the analytical people bring them back to earth by asking for details of how something is going to work, specifically. This is a huge downer for optimistic dreamers, and if not managed properly can quickly cause conflict.

When the group is brainstorming, the systematic personalities fall behind due to their need to analyze every idea thrown into the group pile for consideration. This person must be encouraged to let their "hair down" and enjoy a bit of unstructured discussion.

Optimistic and Outgoing.

This personality type can have difficulty staying within the bounds or scope of a discussion. They are not interested in details, especially details that dampen the outlook of their ideas. Outgoing personalities can align with anyone in the group that seems to support their optimism. If aligned with the dominating personalities in the group, they can be hard to reign in. This alignment only lasts as long as the next new shiny idea, and only if the dominating and confident personality supports the new shiny object.

Outgoing and optimistic personalities tend to be in sales. This means they are persistent and skilled at selling their ideas. They can get accommodating and humble personality types in their corner even if the idea is not supportable with numbers and facts. The optimistic personality can drive the analytical

The  of Satisfaction

personalities in the room crazy.

Humble and Accommodating.

This personality type can often be the smartest people in the room because they have spent much of their time listening and understanding all of the angles. This personality will do almost anything to avoid conflict. In this case, much of the input they have may not see the light of day if not encouraged to participate. This personality type annoys the confident and dominant personality type. The need to be diplomatic in the group setting is more important to them than making sure valuable information breaks through to the group. They will often have discussions, better had in a meeting, in the hallway with a trusted colleague.

All of these personality types can intersect in one person. Some people have a little bit of all of the traits in them depending on the situation. The fact is that we all have dominant traits of one of the types of personalities no matter which model you use or how you define the traits.

The key to successful teams and making emotional connections is understanding that people with particular personality traits act differently to similar situations. Even if you have never seen a Briggs Meyer personality chart, or any other of the hundreds of charts, the concept is the same. Reading people quickly is a skill, and can help you to be successful if you understand and react to them correctly. Simply by being observant in life, this skill can be developed informally. Actually. I believe people that have developed the skill to build emotional connections, have developed the skill through human observations and being situationally aware.

When a customer calls into a call center with a problem or issue, understanding the type of personality you are dealing with is a major skill to master that will make you successful in handling calls. In face to face sales, the ability to read a customer, and adjust during a conversation quickly, will put that prospect or customer at ease and will lower the barrier and cycle of that sale. In life knowing there are certain personality types will help to develop more satisfying relationships when you know what type of personality traits someone has, and what behaviors make them more comfortable. You will be able to adjust your approach to fit their personality.

I want to be clear that I am not advocating for changing who you are as a personality. I am simply suggesting the more we know what makes people tick, the more successful we can be making an emotional connection with them.

The  of Satisfaction

The  of Satisfaction

Making Emotional Connections

It is important to demonstrate and practice skills in order to become a master. I will illustrate what we have been discussing in scenarios that will be familiar to you. I will break out examples and analyze why it is important to make these heartfelt connections with our customers. You can take the details of these examples and apply them to your specific scenarios in your organization. These examples will demonstrate how you can improve your ability to make connections in sales, service & life.

Emotional Connections in Sales

To be successful in sales, it is important to execute the skills we have discussed if you want a successful, long term career. It is possible to sell without creating an emotional connection. People sell things every day without using this approach, but the sales never get easier, or they reach a plateau, and it seems harder and harder to get new sales. The more complex a product or service is, the more important making a personal connection is. The more expensive a product or service is, the more important a connection is. The more successful you want to be in sales, the more important an emotional connection is.

Let's break down a typical inbound sales call and apply the skills of making an emotional connection. In this example we will use a generic call to set up a service. I will use a business to consumer model although you can use this process for business to business as well.

The Greeting

The greeting we use when a potential customer calls is critical to set the tone of the call. If we don't nail the greeting, every time on every call, we will impact our sales numbers in a negative way. No matter what the customer's attitude is on the other end of the line, the tone of the call is set by your attitude. I have observed this phenomenon hundreds of times where the sales person gets a call from a belligerent, difficult, ornery, defensive customer, and immediately loses control of the call by matching the customer's attitude. This is almost always fatal to the call, and if it isn't, it takes twice the work to recover from this mistake.

The way we handle calls that begin in this manner is to respond with the utmost kindness, helpful, and understanding attitude you can deliver. As a sales person you should immediately strategize in your mind that I must diffuse this with a kindness and empathy in your voice, as if you were responding to a 911 call where someone was dying. This customer has done you a great favor broadcasting their distrust of sales people,

The  of Satisfaction

past bad experience with a salesperson, or general misery with the world. This is truly a blessing because they have given you an advantage that will determine what technique you must use to overcome this customer's objection to dealing with sales people or your organization.

If a potential customer broadcasts their disdain of sales people from the beginning, utilize this as a challenge to make a sincere connection with this person. As you begin this call knowing the challenge you have ahead, start by asking questions, and creating an experience that will completely change their mind about sales people. Before you even utter a word, your strategy must be developed, and the delivery and tone of your response must not affirm their pre-conceived perception of a "typical" or "stereo typical" sales person.

Do you remember our discussion about "Situational Awareness"? Do you remember our discussion about "Active Listening"? Do you remember our discussion about "Empathy"? Do you remember our discussion about "Inflection"? Do you remember our discussion about being "Genuine"? Do you remember our discussion about "Sincerity"? Do you remember our discussion about "Timing"? Do you remember our discussion about "Honesty"? Do you remember our discussion about "Enthusiasm"? Every aspect of what we discussed is utilized in the greeting.

Sales Person (SP): "Thank you for calling XYZ Company, my name is Rich, how may I help you set up your services today?" (said with enthusiasm, and a genuine tone of caring)

CX: "I am looking around at services and I really don't like your company, but it looks like you have a decent deal compared to your competitors. I need some prices and details about the deal." (said with disdain, skepticism, and defensiveness).

How would you respond? How do your sales people respond? Do they read from a script? If so the sales person has just validated the stereo type the customer brought to the call. Scripts are the death of sales people and customer service reps. Scripts are a lazy way to train people to sell or serve. Utilizing guidelines or specific legal terms where necessary is fine, but not to control the entire conversation.

The response to the potential customer needs to be delivered with genuine concern, and empathy in the salesperson's voice. The words that are chosen must include an acknowledgement of the customer's dislike of the company at a minimum. It should also include an acknowledgement of the fact that the customer has interest in a deal your organization is offering. And finally, the salesperson must set an expectation of the experience this customer can expect from the sales person on this call. The response must not sound

The  of Satisfaction

scripted and could be approached in a number of different ways. My example below is not the only way, but it includes all of the necessary components.

SP: "I am really sorry to hear that you feel this way about our company. I will be happy to share the details of the deal you are interested in, but first would you share with me why you feel this way about our company?, Again, my name is Rich, who do I have the pleasure of speaking with? (said with true empathy and being completely genuine)

CX: "Joe"

SP:" Nice to meet you Joe! (Transition to acknowledging what the customer said)

This acknowledgement of the customers "dislike" of the company tells the customer a number of things about this salesperson. The first is that he/she is listening to what they said. The second thing this shows the customer is that the salesperson cares about why they feel this way and wants to know more. The wanting to know more is critical in creating this initial connection. It shows the customer the salesperson is not afraid, and is not attempting to hide anything about the company. It is a beginning bridge to building trust.

It is not simply the words this sales person has used but it also matters the way they say the words they choose to use. The tone must be empathetic. Empathy is putting yourself in someone else's shoes, and feeling what that customer must be feeling. Empathy must be genuine. If this salesperson is reading an empathy statement from a script, and they do not feel it in their heart, the statement will fall flat. There are a number of things to consider here. The salesperson should be leaning into the phone focused entirely on the words of the customer. No distractions. No reading e-mails. No flipping through screens to move the process along.

At this point if we have made a successful first step in the connection with the customer, they will most likely share the information because they are convinced that the salesperson actually cares about why they feel this way about the company. Understanding this customer's perception of the company is critical to creating a successful outcome for the salesperson, customer, and the company.

Based on what the customer shares with the salesperson will determine where this conversation must be taken. We have only just begun the call, and already we can see how many critical skills must be used to create a trustworthy connection with the customer in order to be successful. We are a minute into the call, and if it is not handled properly by the salesperson, the outcome is jeopardized. I would argue it could be doomed. So let's continue the interaction.

The  of Satisfaction

CX: "I have a friend that has used your service and says you don't care much about your customers. She says that you have raised her prices over time, and even though she still thinks your price is good, she doesn't feel like your company cares. You are just too big to care about your customers."

What are the key things the customer has revealed here that need to be considered and addressed? Before moving forward go back and re-read what the customer said, and think about what you would key in on, and respond to the customer.

It is important here to understand the customer has not had a problem with your company, but rather they have been told information by a friend that uses the company. This cannot be discounted as hearsay, or just treated as "your friend doesn't know what they're talking about." It is critical for the sales person to address it properly to begin to change this customer's perceptions based on the sales person's response, not their friend. Think about how important referrals are to a business. Many sales come from other customer's experience with your company. A friend tells a friend that they must buy your product. Extremely powerful. The same power is there when a friend tells a friend of a bad experience. It must be addressed and overcome before proceeding.

The next issue is price, but if you look at what the customer says here, they almost overcome that objection before finishing their comment. It should be addressed, but should not become a distraction to the real issues. The other key component of the customer's statement is that the company is too big to care. This perception is often used by customers even though it may not have any relevance to their past experience. Every size company has people that don't care. The thing with big companies is that the perception is easier to stick because in a customer's mind, it makes sense. Some really big companies provide excellent service to their customers. And there are many small companies that provide really lousy service to their customers.

So the response to this customer statement must be delivered very strategically by the salesperson. If you were to coach a sales person to respond, how would you acknowledge this statement? Here is the statement again:

CX: "I have a friend that has used your service and says you don't care much about your customers. She says that you have raised her prices over time, and even though she still thinks your price is good, she doesn't feel like your company cares. You are just too big to care about your customers."

Here is my suggestion for a response to build an emotional connection with the customer.

The  of Satisfaction

SP: "It is really important to have friends you can count on to help you make a good decision, and it is great to hear that your friend thinks our prices are competitive, and the best in our industry, I would like to share with you a few comments and experiences some of my customers have shared with me if that's OK?, (without pausing) and I would ask you to please apologize to your friend on my behalf about any issues they may have had with us. I assure you that my goal today is to show you we care about you and your business."

What do you think? Would you have said it differently? Let's analyze it.

The response starts with a compliment. Compliments are by their very nature a great way to build rapport and connections. Whenever we have the opportunity to compliment we should use it. *"It is really important to have friends you can count on to help you..."* says to that person you make great choices in friends because they can be counted on. This immediately takes away any chance of the customer getting defensive about supporting their friend. The focus on the positive parts of the customer's response lays a great foundation to transition into sharing positive testimonials with the customer. We have not said this customer's friend is wrong, we acknowledge her experience through the apology, but this approach will open the customer's mind to hear what you have to say.

By highlighting the positive points the friend made, competitive pricing, best pricing in the industry, reinforces the pricing advantage. It reminds the customer of why they called in the first place. This is followed by a sincere, empathetic apology, recognizing the friend had a bad experience, but as a sales person we are not afraid of facing issues head on and not running from any accountability.

Finally, the reset of the agenda for the call which is to show this customer they will be making the right decision to use the company's service.

Do you see any additional opportunities to put this customer at ease and to increase the odds of making this a successful call?

So now we need to transition into learning what the customer interests are and how we can satisfy their interests. How do we do that? Ask questions.

Discovering Customer/People Interests

To be effective in sales, the emotional connection is paramount to make a sale. If there is no connection, there will be no sale. People will walk away and come back later if they do not connect with you. Think about the last time you went to buy a car at a car dealership.

The  of Satisfaction

You drive into the parking lot and there are a half dozen sales people standing there ready to pounce on you when you get out of the car. This is a make or break moment for the sales person, and whether or not they will become the person you use to purchase your car.

The only sales people my wife and I have ever worked with are the sales people we connect with. This need to connect with the sales person increases with the price/value of the product or service. Customers never buy based on the price, they buy based on the value. Let me say that again; customers don't buy based on the price, they buy based on the value. This is a critical point to understand.

If we as consumers only bought products and services based solely on price, we would all be wearing the same shoes, drive the same car, and live in the same home. Let me share an example to make the point a bit more clearly.

How much are you willing to spend on a new guitar? If you don't play guitar you will probably not spend a nickel on a guitar. But if you are like me, someone that plays guitar and writes songs for pleasure, you value a good guitar. I have a number of guitars and I am willing to spend a $1000 plus on a guitar, and if my wife let me it would be much more because I treasure writing music on the guitar. This is an example of need based value.

Now if you take two guitar players and ask this same question of them: how much are you willing to spend on a new guitar? Do you think those two guitar players will choose the lowest priced guitar or the best guitar for the value?

A professional musician that uses a guitar for his/her trade, can spend thousands of dollars on a guitar. My interests being more of a hobby, determine how much I am willing to pay for a new guitar. I am not going to buy the hundred dollar guitar, but it is not justified for me to buy a five thousand dollar guitar. I land in the ball park of $800 - $1200. There are a lot of guitars in that range so how do I choose? I ask a lot of questions and play a lot of guitars before buying. That is what a consumer does in every sales decision with every product or service.

Let me share a few more examples. Some people love shoes, and have dozens of pairs for every occasion. I have one pair that I wear out until they shine no more. I buy $60 shoes.

Some people love to run or bike, and they will pay top dollar for their sneakers or bike. I have a bike from Walmart and sneakers from Kohl's. I don't find the value in spending a lot of money, because I don't value them the same way a runner or biker does.

Do you see what I mean when I say we buy based on value? Think about the purchases you make in your life

The  of Satisfaction

and try to apply this concept.

The key to success in selling successfully is to be emotionally connected to what makes our customer tick when it comes to the value they place on the product or service we sell.

So how do we find out what our customer's value? We ask questions and then listen for key phrases and queues that help us determine what our customers value.

Sales people must practice the "Socratic Method", or simply the art of using questions. It is a skill that needs to be understood, developed, and practiced in order to be effective at mastering the technique. It is an excellent method to "control" the sale, and help the customer determine why the product/service is perfect for them.

How do we use questions to sell a product/service that a customer doesn't understand? Shouldn't we just tell them about our product/service so they can determine whether or not they need the product? What happens if we let the customer decide if the product/service is right for them? How can we persuade the customer to buy if we are using questions as our technique to sell?

Let's look at our current example and continue into this discovery stage of the sales process. For this scenario we need to pick a product or service. You can insert your product or service here to make it relevant to you. This process works with every product or service, and it strengthens the emotional connection we make with our customers because the questioning method shows we care about our customer, by finding out what they truly value, and aligning our product or service to the things they value.

Continuing the example interaction:

CX: "I have a friend that has used your service and says you don't care much about your customers. She says that you have raised her prices over time, and even though she still thinks your price is good, she doesn't feel like your company cares. You are just too big to care about your customers."

SP: "It is really important to have friends you can count on to help you make a good decision, and it is great to hear that your friend thinks our prices are competitive, and the best in our industry, I would like to share with you a few comments and experiences some of my customers have shared with me if that's OK?, (without pausing) and I would ask you to please apologize to your friend on my behalf about any issues they may have had with us. I assure you that my goal today is to show you we care about you and your business."

The  of Satisfaction

The transition into discovering the customer's interests:

SP: "Joe, which would you like to hear about first, what customers say about our service or price?"

This transition question gives the customer a choice, and depending on how the customer answers is important to the line of questioning the sales person should pursue. If the customer says they want to hear about the service, it means they are value driven at this point. If the customer says they want to hear about the price, as the sales person you need to understand how price conscious this customer is. Still we need to remember even if they say price, we must find out what they value.

CX: "I would like to know more about your service."

It is very important that as sales people we do NOT jump in and just start throwing features and benefits about our service at the customer. We are still in the trust building part of our interaction, and we need to continue to develop deeper emotional ties with the customer. Using the customer name judiciously from this point on is important to continue building a connection with the customer.

SP: "I will be happy to describe some of the important feature/benefits. In order to make sure I hit the key features/benefits I will need to ask a few additional questions. Joe, how do you expect you will use this product/service in your daily life?"

I have used a general question here to begin the conversation but depending on your product or service you would be more specific. For example, if you are selling computer software that handles inventory you might begin with: *"In order to help me determine where to begin, what is your current inventory software not doing that you wish it was?"*

There are many variables to the route you would take here. If you are selling a consumer product like internet you may begin with a simple question similar to: *"What do you currently use the internet for?"*

The key point is to understand the customer through questioning. As salespeople we must ask enough questions to truly understand what is driving the customers buying/shopping decision. It is also extremely important to personalize the conversation wherever you can to build the emotional connection with the customer. For example: If the customer answered the internet question by saying, *"I work from home."* Your follow up would be similar to, *"What type of business are you in?"* Depending on the answers, and the customer, you might follow up with, *"That's an interesting business, how did you get involved in that industry?"*

The  of Satisfaction

To build a connection we must get to a personal level and truly be interested in what is important to that customer. Remember that customers buy from people that they trust first, and if they like you, they will want to choose you to work with if other things are relatively equal. As sales people, we are always trying to make the decision to buy from us easier for the customer. Trust, likeability, knowledge, interest, listening, honesty all make it easier for the customer to do business with us.

In the sales process there can never be enough understanding of our customer. Well, maybe there is, but the idea is that we must make an emotional connection with our customers to be successful. And being successful is not just making the sale. It is making a sale that the customer is comfortable with, and is the right decision for them. This kind of sale will lead to more sales through word of mouth and referrals.

After a thorough understanding of the customer's needs, we must align those needs when we present the offer/solution/product to the customer. We don't need to focus on everything the product/service we sell is capable of – only the features and benefits that will help the customer with the areas they were most interested in. We must also know when including other feature/benefits could be useful for the customer to know, even if they didn't specifically ask about them.

Customers don't know what they don't know, and as experts we must determine based on our questioning, what is important to provide in our offer. This becomes much easier if we have built a strong emotional connection.

The key to success is to build enough trust through asking relevant and thoughtful questions, and the customer knows we have their interests first, not ours. We become the trusted confidant only when we build the emotional connection with the customer.

Developing the Right Offer

In creating the offer for our customer, we must continue to ensure we have focused on the key areas of the customer's interests. These statements sound like, *"Jim, based on what you told me about your use of the internet, you need to have the fastest speed, this will enable you to do all of your reporting requirements in less time, making running those reports less of a hassle than they are for you today. How does that sound?"*

Based on the answer to the question we may have to ask more questions or simply move forward with the offer. The more complex the product/service we sell, the longer this part of the sales process will be. I am simplifying for purposes of this book, but the connection with our customer can be developed in the

The  of Satisfaction

framework of a twenty minute call or a six month sales cycle. The key is to develop the emotional connection to be successful at sales, no matter what product or service we sell.

In sales there is a common notion that we must ask for the business, and we do. But asking for the business is often anti-climactic when you build a strong connection. If we have taken the time to understand the customer, built a solution based on the customer needs, and tied all of the important features and benefits to the offer, the decision to buy is the logical next step.

But what about pricing? If all of the key areas have been satisfied for the customer, the customer will be focused on the value you created. Remember our discussion on value vs. pricing? The customer is now making a decision based on the value. Any price variance, unless significant, will be less of a hurdle than if we didn't build an emotional connection, and aligned the customer needs to the product/service. In most cases regarding price, when you are negotiating price at this point the sale is done. Pricing is a detail to be worked out, not the main focus of the conversation.

The best sales people are great listeners, and ask a lot of questions. There is a stereo-type that the best sales people are the *"life of the party"*, *"outgoing and always on stage"*, and although there are sales people with these qualities, being a great listener, and the ability to make an emotional connection, is the real key to success. Sales people that are interested in knowing more about people, by asking questions, are always successful at sales. As long as you genuinely care about people, you can be successful in a sales career. Even if you consider yourself a "quiet person", as long as you use the skills of being an "Emotional Connector", you can be the best sales person in the company.

Emotional Connections in Service

I want to share with you a dirty little secret everyone should know. This secret alone may be worth the price of this book. That secret is: we are all in sales. It doesn't matter what business you are in or what role you play, you are in sales. The sooner you understand that reality, the more success you will have in life. There are different degrees in which we each need to be sales people, but in some aspect of your life, you are selling something. It may be a product or a service. It may be an idea that you think will make the company more efficient. It may be an improvement to your company's software. Or it may simply be that you need to sell yourself for your next career position.

In the customer service world, we are "selling" empathy. Since the nature of customer service and retention is to solve customer issues, we need the

The  of Satisfaction

customer to understand we do care, and we genuinely want to help them resolve their issue. We genuinely want our customers to remain a customer, with us or our company.

The emotional connection is a critical component of being a successful customer service professional. Whether you take customer service or retention calls over the phone or provide service face to face, if you make a genuine connection, you will enjoy your position more, and be more successful at providing exceptional customer service.

As is the case with sales, the greeting is the first impression a customer has with you, and you will be judged the second you open your mouth on the phone or make eye contact when you are in person. Let's focus on the phone first.

The Greeting (Phone)

In customer service, the nature of the business is we handle issues for the customer. In most circumstances we are handling an issue where something went wrong. It could be a process. It could be a technical glitch. It could be an incorrect billing statement. It is universal that most calls to customer service are not just to tell the company they are doing great. Although that happened once, it is not the majority of calls. With this in mind, it is common to have customers call that are irritated, and often angry. If they have waited in a queue for any length of time, the expectation is the customer is going to come in "hot". I often use this term "hot" when I am training agents. I use it to describe customers that want to rip your head off the second you finish your greeting, and sometimes before you finish your greeting. It is critical to use the components of an emotional connection flawlessly in these situations.

As we discussed in an effective sales greeting: Do you remember our discussion about "Situational Awareness"? Do you remember our discussion about "Active Listening"? Do you remember our discussion about "Empathy"? Do you remember our discussion about "Inflection"? Do you remember our discussion about being "Genuine"? Do you remember our discussion about "Sincerity"? Do you remember our discussion about "Timing"? Do you remember our discussion about "Honesty"? Do you remember our discussion about "Enthusiasm"? Every aspect of what we discussed so far is utilized in the customer service greeting. There are many similarities, and a few differences.

Customer Service Person (CSP): "Thank you for calling XYZ Company, my name is Rich, how may I assist you today?" (said with enthusiasm, and a genuine tone of caring)

The  of Satisfaction

Customer (CX): "I received a bill from you today and it doesn't have the $50.00 credit on the bill I was promised from the last agent I spoke with. This is the third month in a row this has not been fixed and I just want to cancel my service. You people don't care about me. I have been with you for ten years and the prices just keep going up and the service keeps going down. I am done with you! (said with anger and frustration and screaming)

This is a customer we have all had to work with, right? You can hear the voice in your head as you read this, and you get a little squirmy thinking about it. So what is the right response here? Do we start with a commitment to fix the bill? Do we apologize for the other agents mishandling of the issue? Do we address why the prices have gone up?

We will do all of these at some point, but what this customer really wants is to be heard right now. To know they are being heard. To know they have someone on the phone that can help them, will help them, and will make them feel like their business is important to the company. They are looking for an advocate within the company they can count on.

Based on what we know about making an emotional connection, what would be a good response to begin the healing process for this customer? Let me try, and you see what you think. Actually before you read mine, why don't you formulate your response in your head to see if we are in tune. I will wait.

CSP: "May I have the invoice number please?"

If this was your response I need you to flip back to page one, and start the book over. I would have failed to make my point. If this was the agent's response, and believe me it happens all of the time in customer service centers around the world, the customer's hair would catch on fire, and the screaming would begin or the customer would hang up. Let's try again.

CSP: "I am so sorry to hear that your bill is still incorrect, I know how frustrating this can be and I can hear how frustrated you are, I want to hear all of the details so I can ensure you I will get this fixed for you today. As a matter of fact, as a customer of ten years, and thank you by the way, I have been here for that long and I appreciate your business, I will see what kind of courtesy credit I can get you when we are done as a token of appreciation for your years of loyal service. If you don't mind, can you share the details with me? And again my name is Rich, who do I have the pleasure of speaking with?"

Let's analyze this approach to the greeting. What do you think?

If you run a call center, help desk, retention center

The  of Satisfaction

where you have new agents due to high attrition, pay, burnout, etc, you are thinking my agents could never learn to respond like that. Maybe, but the bigger question is: why do you have people handling your customers that couldn't formulate a response like this?

The customer is legitimately angry due to an ongoing issue created by the agents of the company. We MUST acknowledge it immediately and take responsibility. If we fail here we may never recover. If the customer doesn't believe you understand the issue, and the frustration over it, they will continue to remind the agent of the issue. So for example, when I used the first sample response, *"May I have your invoice number please?"*, no matter how nice you say that phrase, the customer has no confidence you heard anything they said. They will rewind at an even more frustrated level and say something like: *"Did you hear anything I said? I told you that my bill…"*. And they will repeat the entire scenario again, escalating the anger over the issue.

Making an emotional connection is the key to handling all human interactions in life. I believe it so deeply I am writing this book about it! So when we respond to customers in this state, we must connect and empathize. Empathy is the act of putting yourself in the other person's shoes, because you have been there as well. We have all had bad experiences, and we need to remember how frustrating it can be not to be heard.

As the response continues, it is important to recognize the loyalty of our customers. If it was important for the customer to speak to their length of time with the company, it is important for us to recognize the fact. The customers say things for a reason. Especially at the beginning of a call, in the opening statement, the customer will give you all of the information that is important to them. This is especially true in the customer service and retention roles. So even though the response may seem long, it addresses what the customer says, making it clear to the customer that they were heard.

The real emotional connection comes when we can make a conversation with a customer more personal. In the response the connection is deepened with the words, *"...As a matter of fact, as a customer of ten years, and thank you by the way, I have been here for that long and I appreciate your business."* Making it personal if you can, honestly, will start to build the connection with the customer. *"I do appreciate the fact that you have been paying my salary."* This statement sets up the conversation to continue down a path that can get incrementally more personal. As you sprinkle in (remember timing), bits of these connections, at the right time, there will be a moment when you can make a deeper connection. You first must diffuse, and acknowledge the customer. As you continue to build

The  of Satisfaction

trust and confidence with the customer, you can ask more personal questions to make a better emotional connection.

The additional outreach of offering a credit may or may not be something that can be done at your organization. But if you have small "tokens" of appreciation, they should be used accordingly, and ONLY when warranted. We should only use credits when truly appropriate. If we make a strong connection, credits are often not necessary, but can be beneficial to keeping profitable, long term customers.

Asking the customer for the details of what has happened may seem like you're opening the "can of worms" again, and pouring salt over the wound. But in the right circumstances, and in most cases, the customer will appreciate that you want to understand their situation to be helpful. This entire approach must be done with the right tone and genuineness. If you sound like you are scripted, you mine as well just ask for the invoice number.

Getting all of the right information by asking about the situation, is a great way to begin the discovery/questioning process to make sure you can offer the right solution. Transitioning with a name exchange really starts to diffuse the customer, and begin down the path of healing.

What do you think about this response? Does it make an emotional connection with the customer? Do you think it will work at your organization? Do you have a better response?

The most important thing to understand is that the opening greeting sets the foundation for a successful interaction with the customer. The "greeting" does not end at: "How may I assist you today?" The greeting is the opening said with enthusiasm and genuineness, acknowledging and/or empathizing, and exchanging names. Until we know what the customer has called for and we acknowledge it, we are still in the greeting. The greeting does not end until we have responded to the initial customer response.

The Greeting (In person)

When we deal with customers face to face, everything we discussed above is valid, but we add a few additional components to the greeting. We must make eye contact, and use embracing body language.

If the customer in the above scenario walked into any retail customer service desk with the same issue, the exact same words could be used. The additional thing to consider, with a customer right in front of you, is they will watch every move you make to determine if you truly care about their issue. Your eyes and body will give you away if you are not genuine. You need to use your situational awareness skills because not only is the

The  of Satisfaction

customer you are handling watching you for clues, everyone around you, including customers, co-workers, and maybe your supervisor are watching you as well. You have the additional opportunity to be a role model for exceptional customer service. If you think you're only helping the customer at the desk, you're not. When you provide exceptional customer service, and three other customers are watching, they will be impressed, and spread the word if you handle the situation with the skills we have discussed.

Make sure you use the appropriate tone, smile when appropriate, nod in acknowledgement, keep strong eye contact, like that customer is the only person in the world, and lean forward when the customer is speaking to you.

Discovering/ Uncovering Customer Root Reasons for Issues

In the above example, we have started to make the transition to the discovery period by getting the customer to explain the details of the situation. As the customer explains the situation, there will be additional questions needed to uncover why the issue was not resolved. If we don't ask the right questions that are designed to uncover the root cause of why an issue happened, the customer can end up in the same situation over and over again. Just fixing an issue is never enough. We must always be looking to solve the complete issue, and not just band aid the issue. This process will create a greater connection with the customer, and will strengthen the emotional connection, because you are taking the time to get to the bottom of the real issue. This approach builds confidence, trust, and the willingness of the customer to remain a loyal customer. If we don't care, how can we expect our customers to continue to show their caring by using our product or service?

Continuing the Example:

Customer Service Person (CSP): "Thank you for calling XYZ Company, my name is Rich, how may I assist you today?" (said with enthusiasm, and a genuine tone of caring)

Customer (CX): "I received a bill from you today and it doesn't have the $50.00 credit on the bill I was promised from the last agent I spoke with. This is the third month in a row this has not been fixed and I just want to cancel my service. You people don't care about me. I have been with you for ten years and the prices just keep going up and the service keeps going down. I am done with you! (said with anger and frustration and screaming)

CSP: "I am so sorry to hear that your bill is still incorrect, I know how frustrating this can be and I can hear how frustrated you are, I want to hear all of the

The ❤ of Satisfaction

details so I can ensure you I will get this fixed for you today. As a matter of fact, as a customer of ten years, and thank you by the way, I have been here for that long and I appreciate your business, I will see what kind of courtesy credit I can get you when we are done as a token of appreciation for your years of loyal service. If you don't mind, can you share the details with me? And again my name is Rich, who do I have the pleasure of speaking with?"

CX: *"Joan"*

CSP: *"Joan, thank you for that, let's get to the bottom of this. Let's see why the bill is incorrect?"*

CX: *(CX may begin to help with the details and the agent will validate the information in the system. If they do provide more information: listen, acknowledge and thank them!)*

CSP: *"What has been your overall experience with our company for the past 10 years? What are your favorite programs on our channel line up? I love that one too!"*

Based on the product or service, you want to ask questions that you can build rapport around, and deeper connections. If you are selling an internet, TV/Cable service, you can use commonality of interests to build the emotional connection: *"I have the same speed and I love it because I can download my movies faster. How do you like the speed?"*, *"I love the Walking Dead too, which episode has been your favorite this season?"* These questions lead to opportunities to continue the connection and trust with the customer.

Once an agent learns about the issue, it needs a solution. The solution must be aligned with what was discovered, and if it has been an ongoing issue, should include a follow up by you. If that is not the organization's process, you can at least set the expectation for the customer that someone else will follow up. Being transparent about the way the process works also builds trust with the customer.

The emotional connection is part of the interaction with the customer. It is not a standalone skill. It is how we incorporate the human behavioral skills we learn throughout life in every transaction.

Every interaction we have, with each individual we encounter, is similar but different every time. Depending on the situation, it is important we apply each of the appropriate behaviors, at the right moment in the interaction, to build the connection with our customer. We don't use empathy when it is not called for. That undermines being genuine. We don't use enthusiasm when we learn someone has died. That shows we don't care or we weren't listening. Making the emotional connection is an art and science. We need to apply it appropriately. It can seem so simple, and

The  of Satisfaction

make common sense, but it is too often missing in too many interactions.

In sales, retention, and service, there is a known gap in the use of genuine connections with customers. Maybe people just hate their jobs. Maybe people just don't care. Maybe some people are not brought up to understand the importance of the ability to make connections with people. Whatever it is, the business world has a shortage of people that understand the value of an emotional connection.

This is a great opportunity for leaders like you to incorporate this into your culture. Often the reason emotional connections are not made, is because we don't develop our people and coach them on the importance of these skills. People are a reflection of their leadership. So if they don't care, what does that say about their leadership? I believe everyone wants to do a good job, but if there is no expectation to do a good job, or if we don't coach people to get better at their job, who is to blame? Be the leader that helps his/her team to be Emotional Connectors.

I believe that making a connection with people is much easier when people have a common background. There have been price saving moves over the years to move call centers, service centers, and customer facing operations to less expensive offshore locations. If making connections with customers improves our effectiveness in sales and service, how effective can this strategy be? That is a question leaders must ask themselves before making that decision. It could impact their brand reputation negatively.

Most offshoring is motivated by cost. The drive to improve the bottom line at many organizations has put customer service in the back seat. If the CEO's that outsource their customer facing services to other countries understood the power of creating an emotional connection with their customers, and how it drives revenue, they would think twice. There actually is evidence that customer facing organizations have reestablished their customer service operations back within the markets of their customers.

There is an Ally Bank commercial that uses the slogan "we treat you like you would treat you." It is brilliant! It has a person calling a customer service agent that is them, and they connect immediately. Same enthusiasm, same interests, same everything, and it illustrates in one minute the power of the emotional connection! I had to write a book to try to explain it. Thank you Ally Bank!

The failure of outsourcing/offshoring has been and will always be a lack of understanding the power, and importance of a personal connection on the ability to serve customers profitably. When customers call a customer service center, and get a person on the other

The  of Satisfaction

end of the phone that can't "connect" with them because they don't understand the people they are serving, customers feel the company doesn't care about them, only profits. And they would be right. Some cultures just don't make the same types of personal connections the same as others, and some people/cultures place a different value on making emotional connections. This is a global phenomenon, not specific to the United States. The answer is to serve your customers the way they expect to be served. It is simple but often overlooked.

The failure of organizations to provide exceptional customer service and organizational wide customer experiences, is the lack of knowing how to drive people to want to provide excellent service to their customers. It is hard work, and a culture must be built in order to achieve it. Every person in the company must be focused on the customer experience, no exceptions. One person can become a cancer. The company needs to make every interaction with everyone they meet a true genuine connection. The power of having an organization of people that instinctually build connections with each other may seem impossible, but would be utopia in my eyes. There are organizations that try to focus on culture, but it is often undermined by a lack of genuineness toward the goal. People fake their commitment to the cause, and like I stated earlier in my phone example, people can spot a fake a million miles away.

As a sales, retention, or service professional, you should be able to make an emotional connection every interaction. If you can, you will be successful beyond your dreams. If you don't like dealing with people, you should find work that has limited contact with humans. But in today's collaborative work environments that may be difficult. You need to find a way to like working with people.

If you find working with people difficult, try some of these methods to make it easier:

Make it a game – By making the interactions with people a game, you can keep your eye on the goal of the game, and not worry so much about how much you wish you didn't have to work with "Rich" in cubicle 58. Think about it this way: When I get in this meeting with Rich, I am going to focus on getting the information I need to write the code for the User Interface (UX), and then I get to be alone for two weeks without having to see him! I'm just making it up here and you can too.

Be an actor: I tell people that I am always "onstage" when I am at a client site, at a conference, or in a meeting. I act as if there are cameras watching my every move, and that keeps me focused on making emotional connections. I am not pretending as an actor might, I am using this method to focus on my behaviors, and how they are being perceived. I have

The  of Satisfaction

been doing that my entire life. I think it comes from my Catholic upbringing, and the guilt that comes along with that. You can use it to get through those difficult times when you have to interact with people when you don't want to.

Schedule alone time: Make sure you have time to be alone. I find alone time rejuvenating to my soul. I have assessment conversations with myself, and analyze what's been working and what needs to be changed. Being alone is very comforting for most people, but make sure you don't avoid necessary time with people just because you would rather be alone. You have to get out there and talk with people or you will be labeled "not a team player", and that will hurt your career.

Try These Behaviors Every Day to Become an Emotional Connector

In life you can start making emotional connections immediately by doing just a few key things when you meet people. You need to practice and exercise your mind to be good at this, as in any effort worthy of doing and sustaining.

- Smile and look into people's eyes. Use a warm glance as if you have just seen your newborn child or grandchild for the first time.

- When you shake someone's hand for the first

time, hold the shake just a moment longer, look in their eyes and say, *"it is an absolute pleasure to meet you, "Mike" has told me so many great things about you."*

- The next time you walk into a coffee shop, look around and make eye contact, smile, and greet the counter person with a genuine *"hello, how is your day going today"* and then listen and respond accordingly.

- Start all of your conversations in a meeting, family gathering, group, by complimenting the person you are speaking with. *"Emily, that was a very informative update you gave tonight, thank you, I got a lot out of the information you provided."*

- Greet everyone you meet as if this could be the last time you will ever see them again. I use this as a standard because it motivates me to make it a memorable and engaging experience for me. I have been a volunteer for Hospice, and that experience has changed the way I look at life.

- Every day when you walk out the door say to yourself: *"This is going to be a great day!"*

- Be grateful. Run through your mind all of the blessings in your life. Focus on the good, and what one small thing you can do today to make

The  of Satisfaction

someone else's day better. Do this as often as necessary. It will help you to be in the right frame of mind to connect with people.

- Believe you have a purpose. I believe we are all on this earth for a purpose, and everything we encounter has a reason or meaning toward that purpose. It is not always clear what our purpose is, especially when things don't seem to be going well, but knowing it is playing a part to make us better somehow helps. After 57 years on this earth I am still finding and fulfilling my purpose.

- Enjoy the people you work with at every job, even if you absolutely hate the job. Find the purpose in why you are there. It may be to make a lifelong friendship with a co-worker.

- Don't leave a job in haste. If your job pays well and you like what you do, but a boss is giving you a hard time, wait it out. Focus on the things that you can control, and avoid the boss as much as possible. If you can make emotional connections at your job, and you love your customers and co-workers, find a way to stay. If you do leave, be very sure the next place is going to have more opportunity for you to make an impact and meet great people.

- Don't be paralyzed by other people's opinions of you. Have the opinion that you are a good person, trying to be a better person, and will someday be a great person. Know who you are, and keep building genuine emotional connections with the people you meet.

- Open the door for others. Men be chivalrous, and ladies be gracious. If a gentleman opens the door for you, know that it comes from a good place in their heart. Ladies be confident and determined without a chip. After all, you do most things better than men anyway.

- Walk into a room as if it is your stage, and the cameras are watching your every move. Because they are. Everyone watches everyone else very closely to determine who you are. Be someone they would like to connect with.

- Be the giver. The giver of advice (when asked), share wisdom, give your time, expertise and experience. Give money if you can, time if you can't. Think of how you can help others and not how it helps you. Be selfless.

- Pick your head up out of your phone. There are people you need to meet, and they could be standing right in front of you.

The  of Satisfaction

- When someone does something you appreciate, tell them you appreciate what they did, and why.

- When someone you know suffers a loss, be there for them. Even if you have no words, your presence will comfort them. The words will come. Hug to allow tears.

- Treat conversations as an opportunity to learn, not an opportunity to win.

- Stay in touch with people. Call and ask: "how are you doing?" Don't wait until you need something.

- Forgive

Conclusion

I said at the beginning of this book, that by continuing to develop and practice the skills of making an emotional connection, I have been a success in this life beyond my wildest dreams. I believe I have been successful, but I am always learning how to be even better at this life. What I have learned in my 57 years is that it is the small things in life that matter. The things that no one notices: like providing for a family, mentoring your kids to be good people, helping a neighbor in a time of need, making people feel good about who they are, and always ready to help when help is needed. You don't win an Academy Award for any of these activities, but you do leave a positive legacy.

There are many degrees of success, and each person needs to define success for themselves. I define my success this way: *Success to me is being a loving husband that cherishes my wife Justine. I celebrate how lucky I am to have her as a life-long companion. Being the best dad I can be to my two children, Taylor and Emily. I try to be a great role model so they have an example of what a good person can be. I am not perfect, but I think I passed that test. You can ask them. To do what I can to be helpful whenever the opportunity presents itself. Save enough money to never have to take a job I didn't want to just pay the bills. And making other people feel good about themselves after having met me.*

The  of Satisfaction

You will define your success differently. What I do know is that however you define it, making the emotional connection with others will be what you treasure the most in the end. People on their death bed are often very practical about their assessment of the life they lived. They often want to be sure their family is taken care of. They want to believe they are leaving a positive legacy. They don't care much about the jobs they have had, but they do care about the people they have met at those jobs along the way. It is always an assessment of what they did to make their family, friends, and world, a better place while they were here. You can't do that by being alone.

The sales and service professions are the ultimate place to impact lives on a daily basis. It is not just to fix customer issues or make the sale, but it is to help that person feel that someone cared enough to listen and provide what they needed at the time.

Take advantage of the opportunity to be great at making emotional connections. Leave a lasting positive legacy with everyone you meet. We all are going to leave a legacy simply by having been on this earth. Take control of that legacy and start today. Start right now. Smile at someone and say: *"It is a pleasure meeting you today, thank you for making my day better."*

ABOUT THE AUTHOR

Rich Hand is a dedicated husband and proud father of two grown children. He loves writing songs, books, and notes to his family. He cherishes the opportunity to have an audience to speak to about the things he is passionate about. He loves his dogs with all his heart and dreads the day his dogs will need his love to let them go. He knows his heart may not be able to take it. Until then he fills his heart with his best efforts to inspire people to live their life; Ignored!

www.ingramcontent.com/pod-product-compliance
Lightning Source LLC
Chambersburg PA
CBHW060351190526
45169CB00002B/568